THE ANIMAL FAMILY ALBUM

Contents

Bear 6	Sheep 26
Cat 8	Goose 28
Duck 10	Swan 30
Deer 12	Lion 32
Donkey 14	Peacock 34
Fox 16	Pig 36
Elephant 18	Seal 38
Kangaroo 20	Turkey 40
Rabbit 22	Whale 42
Horse 24	Tiger 44

THE ANIMAL FAMILY ALBUM

written and illustrated by Tony Palazzo

edited by Robin Fox

Copyright © 1967 by The Lion Press, Inc. This Young Readers Press, Inc., edition is published by arrangement with The Lion Press, Inc.

2nd printing................October, 1969
Printed in the U. S. A.

BEAR

MOTHER	FATHER	YOUNG	GROUP
SOW	BOAR	CUB	SLOTH

There are many kinds of bears in all parts of the world. They are huge—the Alaskan Kodiak bear is the biggest, and small—you can almost hold the Australian Koala bear in your hands! They are black, brown, white, speckled, or gray. All bears belong to the same family of animals and many of them have the same habits.

Did you know that most bears hibernate all winter? They sleep and doze during the long cold season, never leaving their cozy cave shelters for food. Their bodies have stored energy and fat from many meals of grasses, leaves, fruits, berries, insects, small animals, fish—and especially, honey.

Babies—cubs, usually twins—are born about the middle of winter. They weigh less than one pound, although their mother probably weighs between three hundred and one thousand five hundred pounds! At first, the cubs cannot see and they have no teeth or hair. Their mother nurses them and soon they grow strong and furry.

In the spring the cubs learn how to feed themselves and how to protect themselves. Bears often climb trees for food and to escape danger. Even though they look clumsy, most bears can run very fast for short distances. We think of them as jolly animals, and they are gentle and easily trained to dance and wear funny costumes in the circus.

CAT

MOTHER	FATHER	YOUNG	GROUP
PUSS, QUEEN,	TOM	KITTEN	CLOWDER
or TABBY			

People have written stories, poems, plays and songs about cats. Long ago, in Egypt, one of the most important goddesses had a cat's head and paws!

If they like you, cats are very friendly and playful. They purr, and knead with their front paws when they are happy. Some cats will even lick your hand with their long, rough, pink tongues. But when they are tired, or want to be left alone, they will hide or run away, and you cannot change their minds. If you try too hard, the cat may hiss, puff out its hair so it looks twice as big and *very* fierce. And remember — they do have sharp claws and teeth!

Cats like to be clean, so they lick their fur to keep it soft and shiny. Most housecats eat canned food, and drink milk, but they like to hunt mice, snakes, small animals, and birds.

The mother cat may have six tiny kittens in each litter. Kittens are very cute and funny as they tumble and play.

There are many colors of cats. Some have short hair. Some have long hair. Most have long tails, but some have none! They smell and hear everything, and they see in the dark. Lions, tigers, jaguars, cougars, panthers, pumas, wildcats eat, hunt and do very much the same things that your own kitty does; they are all cousins!

DUCK

|MOTHER|FATHER|YOUNG|GROUP|
|DUCK|DRAKE|DUCKLING|FLOCK|

Ducks are happiest in water. They paddle wherever they find it and quack loudly. They want to be in water even in the winter, and so, when ice covers the ponds, they paddle busily to keep a small place from freezing.

It is always fun to see ducks diving head first for food. They gather mud and water in their flat bills, then strain the bugs and little plants out by swishing their tongues and shaking their heads. Farm ducks eat insects, grubs, grains, and grasses that they find on land. Sometimes, they will steal garden vegetables too, and pester other barnyard animals. When they are chased, how silly they look, waddling and flapping their wings, hurrying for the safety of their pond.

Ducklings hatch from greenish eggs which their mother lays in a nest and then keeps them warm by sitting on them. In stores or on the farm, you see pale-colored powder puffs darting about on tiny yellow feet—they are newly hatched ducklings! Duck eggs are very good to eat, and some farmers raise ducks for eating, too.

Wild ducks swim, eat, and hatch their eggs as their barnyard cousins do. But when fall comes, flocks of beautifully colored wild ducks fly in V-shaped patterns, south. When they return to the fields and woods in the north we know that spring has come.

DEER

|MOTHER|FATHER|YOUNG|GROUP|
|DOE|BUCK|FAWN|BAND|

Deer always watch, and listen, and sniff the air. They must protect themselves from animals who want to eat them, and from men, who hunt them for food and for their soft hides. Sometimes deer escape by running fast on their thin legs, with their lovely small heads pointed into the wind, and their short tails held straight up in the air. But sometimes they stand still as statues and seem to disappear, because they are the same soft brownish, reddish, grayish, and speckled colors as the woods and meadows. Most deer are wild, but in cold, northern countries people use them to pull sleds and wagons.

Small bands of deer—the doe, fawns, and sometimes the buck—wander in the woods, eating grasses, tree bark, and mosses. They use their sharp hooves to break small trees, so that they may eat the tender top leaves.

You may wonder why only a few have tall, bone antlers growing from the tops of their heads. Antlers grow only on bucks, who use them for fighting. Every year the old antlers fall off, and the bucks grow bigger, new ones!

White-tailed deer, moose, red deer, elk, mule deer, caribou, and reindeer are some of the wonderful names of different kinds of deer who live in hot countries and cold countries, in mountains and in fields, all over the world.

DONKEY

MOTHER	FATHER	YOUNG	GROUP
JENNY	JACK-ASS	FOAL	PACE

Poor donkeys!

People call them stupid and stubborn. Ever since the time, long ago, when the Bible was written, donkeys have worked, pushing and pulling, carrying people and heavy loads. Poor donkeys, nobody ever thinks of them as beautiful or nice to have as pets.

The patient donkey climbs narrow mountain trails or rocky paths hardly ever slipping, and he carries heavy packs across hot deserts. *But*, sometimes he stops. He will refuse to move until *he* wants to! Maybe he will even sit down! If you pull him, or try to make him move, he will bray loudly, with his large mouth wide open and his head tossed back. Sometimes, but not often, you can tease and persuade him to get up if you offer him a carrot!

Donkeys, like their cousins—zebras, burros, and horses—graze, eating grasses and grain. Donkeys are smaller than horses and they have shorter manes and much bigger ears. They live in stables as horses do, and they eat hay, apples, and sugar cubes, too. Children often learn to ride donkeys before they ever ride a horse.

But the donkey is a worker, and wherever he lives, there is a job for him. Poor donkey!

FOX

MOTHER	FATHER	YOUNG	GROUP
VIXEN	REYNARD	KIT	PACK

Foxes have thick, soft fur from the tips of their shiny black, pointed noses to the ends of their long, bushy tails. They are hunted all over the world for their fur which is red, or brown, or silver gray, and sometimes even black. The arctic fox has white fur in winter and yellowish fur in summer.

Have you ever heard someone say, "Clever as a fox"? Foxes are sly, cunning —and clever. Hunting dogs follow them by their smell. All animals have special smells, called "scents." By jumping a fence and running a short distance, then jumping back again, the clever fox confuses the hunting dogs who must stop and sniff to find his trail again. And foxes run along the tops of stone walls, too high for the dogs to follow their scent. They will even run in a brook, or swim in a stream—for dogs can never follow a trail in the water! Very foxy!

Foxes make their dens in hollow trees, caves, and in holes they burrow in the ground. They eat small animals, fruit, and berries. But, they eat the farmers' chickens and ducks, too! That is why farmers hunt and set traps for them.

When nighttime comes, foxes often run in packs across the fields and hills in the moonlight looking for food. You can hear them sadly howling, or gaily yipping and barking as they go.

ELEPHANT

MOTHER	FATHER	YOUNG	GROUP
COW	BULL	CALF	HERD

Full grown elephants weigh as much as four or five automobiles put together! A tall man would have to stand on another man's shoulders to see over an elephant's head. The bull elephant has two tusks — actually teeth — which grow out of his mouth. Each tusk weighs as much as a man does. And, elephants live for more than one hundred years!

They fight, work, and eat with their amazing trunks. They pull up flowers and plants and scoop them into their mouths. They drink by sucking water up into their

trunks and emptying it into their mouths. Sometimes they lift their trunks high above their backs and blow the water out for a shower bath — elephant style.

Elephants have no hair on their gray hide — just a few bristles and a whisk at the ends of their thin tails. The babies — calves — are large when they are born, but they stay with their mothers for nearly four years.

Long ago, there were elephants all over the world. But now they live only in Africa and Asia where they are trained to work like bulldozers, pushing, pulling, uprooting trees, and carrying heavy loads. They are very intelligent. Some people say they never forget their jobs — or people!

Every circus has elephants who dance on their hind legs or wear a costume and balance balls with their trunks.

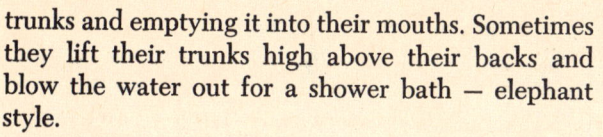

KANGAROO

MOTHER	FATHER	YOUNG	GROUP
FLYER	BOOMER	JOEY	MOB

Kangaroos are special.

No other animal in the world looks like a kangaroo. Its small head and pointed ears make us think of a dog. Its front legs, which dangle above the ground, look a little like arms. But the big hind legs which rest flat on the ground, and the long round tail which stretches out behind, tell us—*kangaroo!*

Many different kinds of kangaroos grow wild on the islands of Australia and Tasmania—and nowhere else in the world! Kangaroos can leap very fast. The giant red or gray kangaroo—taller than a man!—kills its enemies by kicking with strong hind legs and long, sharp, toe-nailed feet, or by swinging its heavy tail like a whip. Tree kangaroos, wallabies, wallaroos, and euros are all kangaroos. There is even a little rat kangaroo which scurries and hops through the grasses.

The mother kangaroo has a furry pocket—called a "pouch"—on her stomach. When her baby is born it is so small you could put it in a teaspoon! The tiny baby — a joey — crawls into the mother's pouch and lives there warm and protected for about six months. When it grows too big, it hops out and joins its mother eating grass and leaping across the wide fields.

RABBIT

| MOTHER | FATHER | YOUNG | GROUP |
| DOE | BUCK | BUNNY or KIT | WARREN |

Every time a farmer plants lettuce, carrots, or other vegetables, he knows that rabbits will try to eat his garden! So he sets traps, he trains his dogs to chase them, and sometimes he hunts rabbits, too.

The wild cottontail rabbit is brownish with a furry, white stomach and a white tail. He usually eats clover, leaves, bark, and grasses. But sometimes he sneaks into the garden for a feast. If the dogs and the farmer are asleep, he eats happily, but if they find him, he must run to safety. Rabbits hide in hollow logs, in piles of rocks, under bushes. If they are near home, they scamper into the underground tunnels they have dug, to be safe inside the cozy burrow. When there is no place to hide the rabbit crouches—hardly breathing. He almost disappears. His brown fur can match the color of hay, sand, grass, or leaves. He waits, never moving until he is safe. With his big ears straight up, he sniffs the air, then—gaily hops away. Rabbits live in almost every country, and everywhere, they are hunted.

Some farmers grow tame rabbits for food. Doe rabbits—the mothers—have three or four litters of bunnies—babies—a year, and there are five or six bunnies in each litter. Many people like the white, black, and spotted fur of tame rabbits for coats, or fur-lined gloves, or slippers.

HORSE

| MOTHER | FATHER | YOUNG | GIRL | BOY | GROUP |
| MARE | STALLION | FOAL | FILLY | COLT | HERD |

Ancient horses were no bigger than dogs! Cavemen hunted and ate them. None of those tiny horses live today, but their relatives do—tame and wild, big and small.

Almost everything you can think of that we do with machines today, our grandfathers did with horses. Imagine, instead of traveling in a train, or in an airplane for just a few hours, sitting for days in a wagon pulled by a horse! Farmers and grocerymen had workhorses, postmen rode fast horses, and soldiers even went to war on horseback.

Horses still work, and there is a different kind of horse for each job. But nowadays we have fun with them, too. Big, slender horses run their fastest, to win races. At horse shows, they try to win prizes for their riders, with their best prancing, galloping, and jumping fences. And what fun it is to watch cowboys and cowhorses at a rodeo! On horseback you can ride high in the mountains to a hidden lake, or deep into the woods where there are no roads.

Sometimes horse's names tell us where they come from—the huge, strong Suffolk comes from England, the friendly, little Shetland Pony comes from the Shetland Islands, and the beautiful Tennessee Walker comes from Tennessee.

Black, brown, red, white, yellow, gray, spotted, or speckled, workhorse, racehorse, or pet—could anything be nicer than a horse?

SHEEP

MOTHER	FATHER	YOUNG	GROUP
EWE	RAM	LAMB	FLOCK or FOLD

Wild sheep and wild goats have straight hair. They roam in mountains and rocky valleys, nibbling leaves and grasses. Wild rams — the fathers — often grow big curved horns which make them look fierce and proud, and not like their tame, timid, woolly cousins — sheep.

The saying "Gentle as a lamb" is true. Sheep and their babies — lambs — are gentle, peaceful animals who do not hunt or kill for food. They graze quietly, close together in flocks. They have thick, curly, creamy white wool, and short legs with little pointed hooves. Their "baa-baa-baa" is sometimes funny, sometimes like crying.

Wool for your pants, sweaters, blankets, and mittens comes from sheep. When their heavy coats are cut off, sheep look skinny and naked. But the thick wool grows back each time it is cut. Lamb, or mutton (as their meat is called) is eaten in almost every country.

Fluffy, new-born lambs, running and playing in fields full of flowers, mean spring is here! Sheep are guarded by a shepherd, a man, sometimes a boy, who lives with the flock. Together with their sheepdogs, shepherds watch for wolves and other animals who hunt sheep.

Many poems, fairy-tales, songs, and stories in the Bible have been written about shepherds and their flocks of woolly gentle, trusting sheep.

GOOSE

MOTHER	FATHER	YOUNG	GROUP
GOOSE	GANDER	GOSLING	GAGGLE

When fall comes, we can see wild geese high in the sky, flapping their wide wings and flying in a V-shaped pattern—pointing south. They return north soon after the robins. They honk and gabble loudly as they fly, telling us spring has really come at last!

Geese live in marshes and swamps. Before the goose—the mother—lays a nest full of eggs, both she and the gander—the father—drop their last year's feathers. This is called "molting," and does not hurt the birds. While geese molt they cannot fly. The new feathers are brightly-colored and shiny.

Ducks and geese both live near water, but geese find most of their food—grubs, and grasses—on land. They are bigger than ducks. Their necks are longer and their bodies fatter. Geese have wide, webbed feet—pink, or white, or black—which they hold close to their bodies when they fly.

Tame geese and ducks waddle together in the barnyard and they are both so good to eat. Not many people eat goose eggs although they are tasty.

Wild and tame geese protect themselves and their babies—goslings—by standing as tall as they can, flapping their wings loudly and making a hissing sound which frightens the enemy off.

Be careful, do not touch their goslings. Geese can nip with their wide, flat bills—and it hurts.

SWAN

MOTHER	FATHER	YOUNG	GROUP
PEN	COB	CYGNET	FLOCK

It looks like magic!

    Swans swim with out moving! Their small heads, with pointed black or orange beaks, are very still. Their long, long, curved necks seem frozen in an S-shape. Look at their bodies — nothing moves. Even the water around them seems still. How beautiful they are—graceful white swans reflected in a lake.

    And yet, swans can swim fast. How do they swim without moving? Under the water, their strong, short legs paddle back and forth. Their large webbed feet, which look so clumsy on land, scoop water behind them and the swan glides on — like magic!

30

Wild swans migrate — flying south in the fall and returning north in the spring along with wild ducks and geese. You can recognize a flock of flying swans because their bodies are as long as their long, slender necks.

Some swans are named for the sounds of their voices. The trumpeter swan has a deep, loud call like a trumpet; the whistling swan coos with a high, whistling sound, and the mute swan's call is soft and low.

Did you know that a swan's feathers never get wet? Water birds, like swans, ducks, and geese, must preen themselves often — take care of their feathers. They spread oil on them with their beaks. The oil comes from tiny pores — holes — near their tails. This preening makes the swans smooth and glistening. And it keeps them from getting wet!

LION

MOTHER	FATHER	YOUNG	GROUP
LIONESS	LION	CUB	PRIDE

Lions have large, strong bodies covered with yellowish-brown fur. Very sharp claws lie hidden in their big paws, and the fathers—lions—have thick manes around their heads like dark collars. When they stand waving their long, thin tails, their shiny yellow eyes glaring—we know why lions are called "the king of beasts."

Lions eat meat. Either alone or in small bands they hunt antelopes, giraffes, and any animal they can catch—sometimes even people. The lion surprises and frightens the hunted animal, and then the lioness—the mother—chases it and kills it. She eats after the lion is full, and finally the cubs—the babies—eat, too.

For almost a year after they are born, cubs stay with their parents and learn how to hunt. At first they just watch, and eat. Later, the cubs hunt alone and their parents watch—sometimes helping with the kill—and then they all eat.

Lions live on wide, open plains in Africa, Asia, and India. The color of their tawny fur hides them as they crouch or snooze in the long grasses. Lions have happy family lives. The rowdy cubs fight and play while their parents watch, dozing in the sun. Circus lions leaping through hoops, sitting on chairs, ducking their trainers' whips, must dream of freedom in the hot, dusty, wild country.

PEACOCK

MOTHER	FATHER	YOUNG	GROUP
PEA HEN	PEACOCK	CHICK	FLOCK

Peacocks are unfriendly birds with loud screechy voices, and nobody hunts them or trains them to do tricks. Just a few people eat peacock pie, and who ever heard of a scrambled peacock egg? *But,* peacocks are kept in parks and zoos. Why?

Peacocks are beautiful. Their bodies are a lovely, special blue, called peacock blue. They have a train of long feathers for a tail. Opened and lifted straight into the air, the train becomes a huge, splendid, jewel-colored fan! What colors! Gold, green, and plum. A big eye-shaped spot of peacock blue glistens at the tip of each feather. The colors catch sunlight as if the whole wonderful tail were made of tiny mirrors!

Peacocks must know how fine they look, because they often open their tails and walk proudly—strutting—showing off. The short, bright feathers on the tops of their small heads bob as they strut. You can almost hear them say, "I'm perfect! Yes I am!" Now you know where the saying "Proud as a peacock" comes from.

The poor pea hen lives a dull life. Nobody looks at her. She is plain, brownish-colored, without a fancy train of feathers. A few completely white peacocks live in zoos—but the bright, wild peacocks live in Asia.

It must be like a dream to see them strutting, tails fanned out, gleaming in the dark, green forests!

PIG

MOTHER	FATHER	YOUNG	GROUP
SOW	BOAR	SHOAT	DROVE

Pigs take baths—mud baths! They crowd into muddy puddles and wallow happily, squealing and waving their fat legs in the air.

When flies and insects crawl over their bristly backs, biting and stinging them, pigs are helpless. They cannot turn their heads around to lick the bugs away. Their necks are too fat and stubby. They scratch their heads with their small, pointed hooves, but their legs are too short to reach and scratch the rest of their bodies. And their little, curled tails are useless as fly swatters, so they take mud baths. Wet mud is cool. When it dries, pigs are "dirty as a pig"—covered with dirt armor.

Pigs will eat *anything!* But on farms where farmers grow pigs to take to market, they are carefully fed on corn, wheat, peanuts, grasses, and milk to make them "fat as a pig." From their jowls—their cheeks—to their feet, their meat, called "pork," is delicious. Ham, bacon, and sausages are made from pork.

Wild pigs are dangerous. When they are angry or guarding their babies—piglets—they chase their enemies. Their fierce little eyes shine. They snort and grunt noisily. And their sharp tusks—long front teeth—point like knives. Most of their enemies run away!

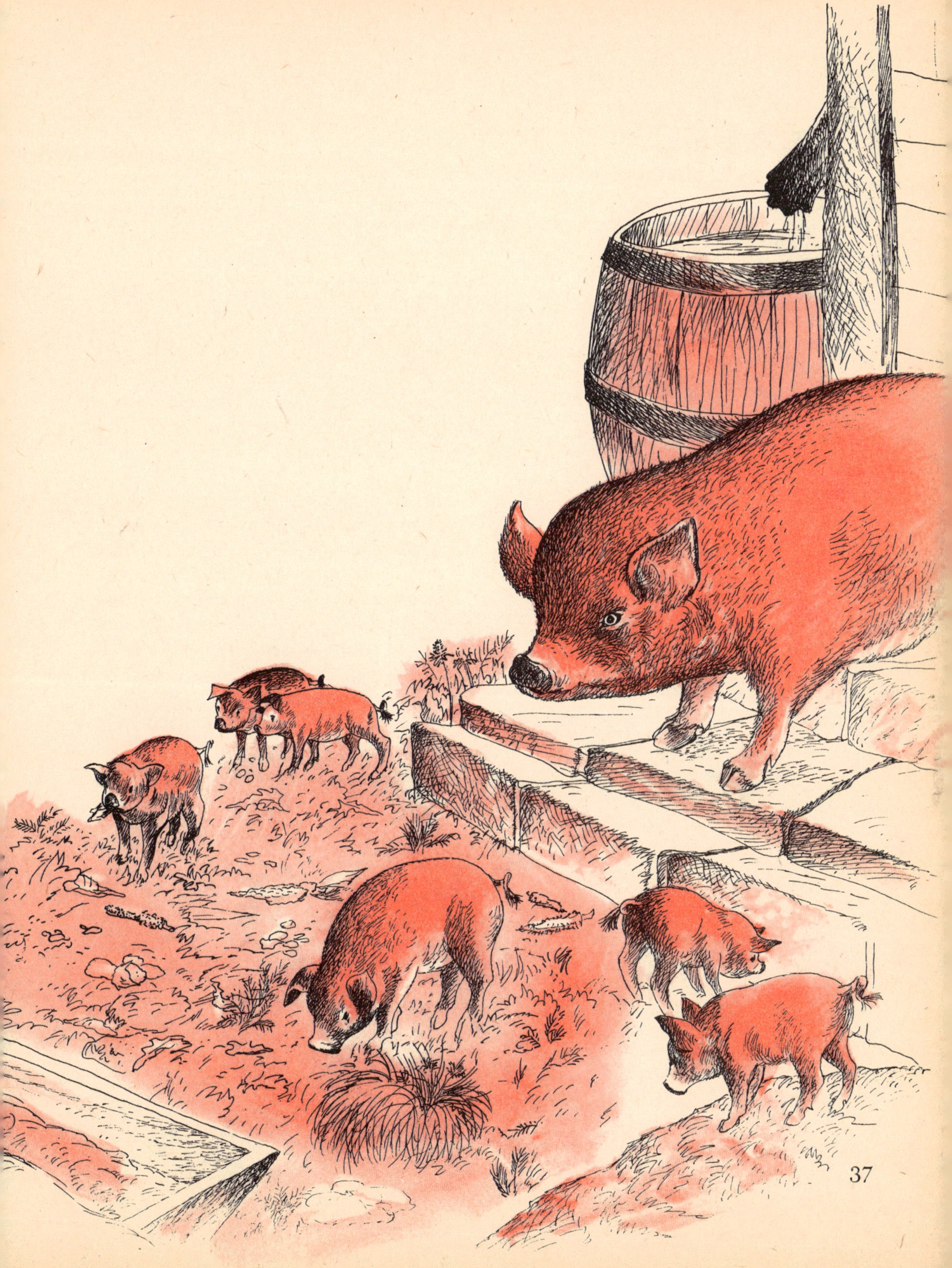

SEAL

MOTHER　FATHER　YOUNG　GROUP
COW　　BULL　　PUP　　TRIP

    Seals and sea lions live strange lives. Cows — the mothers — and their pups — the babies — stay all winter and most of spring along shores where the sea water is warm. Bulls — the fathers — never leave cold, northern water. In June, cows and bulls finally meet on the Pribilof Islands near Alaska, where the pups are born. No one knows why, but most seals swim to these same islands every year!

    The bulls arrive first. When the cows come, there is quite a scuffle. Each bull herds as many cows as he can find for himself, onto a beach. When the pups are born, he guards his many families for several months — never leaving them, *not even to eat!* The cows eat fish, lie in the sun, nurse their pups, and teach them to swim.

Seals are great swimmers but they are awkward on land. They cannot walk. Instead of legs, seals, sea lions, and walruses — their cousins — have two short, flat, front flippers, and a fishlike tail. Their front flippers balance them as they push with their tails, and their heavy bodies lurch and sway as they go.

Eskimos hunt seals for their meat and rich fat — called "blubber." Their short-haired, shiny fur is often made into coats and hats.

Seals are smart, happy animals. They clap their front flippers loudly after their tricks at the circus. They like the show too!

TURKEY

MOTHER	FATHER	YOUNG	GROUP
HEN	GOBBLER or TOM	POULT	FLOCK

    Turkeys have always lived in America. Long before the pilgrims had their first Thanksgiving turkey dinner, the Mexican Aztecs and American Indians hunted and feasted on wild turkeys.

    Today there are many more tame turkeys than wild turkeys in America. Huge turkey farms raise thousands of birds for Thanksgiving and Christmas dinners. Tame turkeys have big, brown bodies and tiny heads perched on top of skinny necks. When they stretch their necks — up and down, longer and shorter — their red wattles shake. Wattles are the flabby skins that hang under their chins. They are something to see as they look for food! They jerk their heads from side to side as they peer at the ground, and with each step they lift their orange feet and claws high off the ground. They say "gobble, gobble, gobble" as they go. How their wattles shake!

    Wild turkeys are smaller than tame ones and all their feathers are brown. They live in fields and woods, hiding from hunters. Tame turkeys cannot hide — they are born to be eaten. Sometimes the gobbler — the father — proudly fans out his tail and shows the white tips at the ends of each feather. Maybe he knows what a good Thanksgiving dinner he makes!

WHALE

MOTHER	FATHER	YOUNG	GROUP
COW	BULL	CALF	(POD) or SCHOOL

Whales breathe air because — they are animals, not fish! But they live deep in the ocean, they never come up on land, they eat fish and seaweed. They are the biggest animals alive — in fact, they are the biggest animals that ever lived!

The huge blue whale, the very biggest of all, weighs as much as twenty elephants. From the tip of his squarish head to the end of his tail he is over one hundred feet long, and smooth, gray, and hairless.

When it is time for the cows — the mothers — to have their calves — their babies — whales swim to the same place each year. A calf weighs as much as two big automobiles when it is born. The cow nurses her calf with enough milk to fill over four hundred bottles a day!

Some whales strain their food — about one ton every day — through fringes of bone in their cave-like mouths, but others strain it through rows of cone-shaped teeth.

Whales stay under water for as long as fifteen minutes. They swim up to the surface to breathe fresh air. They blow out used air and water from a hole in the tops of their heads. This spray of water tells whale hunters where to find them. Whale fat — called "blubber" — is used to make margarine and many other things.

TIGER

MOTHER	FATHER	YOUNG	GROUP
TIGRESS	TIGER	KITTEN	TROOP

Tigers are big and strong. Their orange fur has wavy, black stripes. Their long tails have rings of black all the way to the tips. Their bellys are white and sometimes they have white fur around their glowing, orange eyes which see in the dark. With their small ears they can hear the softest sounds of a trapped, hiding animal's breathing. Inside their paws are long claws, and their teeth are sharp, and gleaming white. When they twitch their stiff whiskers as they lick themselves or sniff the wind, they look like a gentle housecat. But tigers are wild, very fierce animals.

Tigers hunt alone, often at night. They crouch and wait, hidden by their striped coats that match the tall grasses or the bushes stirring in the breeze. When an antelope, monkey, deer, or other animal stops to graze, the tiger flashes out of his hiding place and leaps at the frightened animal. Tigers climb trees, perch on a branch, and drop down on animals that walk below. They are swift runners and almost no animal can get away from them.

When you see tigers snoozing in zoo cages, or sitting on chairs, or leaping through hoops at the circus — close your eyes and try to imagine how proud and beautiful wild tigers are as they stalk through the forests and dark jungles in Asia.